The Roman Empire and its Impact on Britain

Claire Throp

Raintree is an imprint of Capstone Global Library Limited, a company incorporated in England and Wales having its registered office at 7 Pilgrim Street, London, EC4V 6LB – Registered company number: 6695582

www.raintree.co.uk
myorders@raintree.co.uk

Edited by Helen Cox-Cannons and Holly Beaumont
Designed by Richard Parker
Original illustrations © Capstone Global Library Limited 2015
Illustrated by Martin Sanders (Beehive Illustration)
Picture research by Svetlana Zhurkin and Pam Mitsakos
Production by Helen McCreath
Originated by Capstone Global Library Limited
Printed and bound in China by CTPS

ISBN 978 1 406 29107 0 (hardback)
18 17 16 15 14
10 9 8 7 6 5 4 3 2 1

ISBN 978 1 406 29112 4 (paperback)
19 18 17 16 15
10 9 8 7 6 5 4 3 2 1

British Library Cataloguing in Publication Data
A full catalogue record for this book is available from the British Library.

Acknowledgements
We would like to thank the following for permission to reproduce photographs: Alamy: Heritage Image Partnership Ltd, 5, 19, Jeff Morgan 14, 12, Nick Turner, 20, Prisma Archivo, 8, Tim Gainey, 17; Art Resource, N.Y.: The Trustees of the British Museum, 21, 26; Corbis: Arcaid/Jonathan Bailey, 22, Jason Hawkes, 13; Dreamstime: Chris Dorney, cover; Getty Images: UIG, 25, UIG/Environment Images, 16; Newscom: akg-images/Richard Booth, 29, World History Archive, 15; Shutterstock: antb, 14, Chris Hill, cover inset (coin), Claudio Divizia, 11, Hyena Reality, background (throughout), Karramba Production, cover (top left), back cover, Laurence Gough, 18, PLRANG, 23, Richard Semik, 28, Route66, cover inset (gold coin), SimonHS, 27, Stanislav Petrov, background (throughout), Vadim Sadovski, 6—7 (back), wk1003mike, 10; Wikipedia: Immanuel Giel, 9.

We would like to thank Dr Mark Zumbuhl of the University of Oxford for his invaluable help in the preparation of this book.

Every effort has been made to contact copyright holders of material reproduced in this book. Any omissions will be rectified in subsequent printings if notice is given to the publisher.

All the internet addresses (URLs) given in this book were valid at the time of going to press. However, due to the dynamic nature of the internet, some addresses may have changed, or sites may have changed or ceased to exist since publication. While the author and publisher regret any inconvenience this may cause readers, no responsibility for any such changes can be accepted by either the author or the publisher.

Contents

Some words in this book appear in bold, **like this**. You can find out what they mean by looking in the glossary.

Goodbye to the Iron Age

The Romans came from Rome in Italy. Their **empire** included many countries by the time Julius Caesar, a Roman general, **invaded** Britain in 55 BC.

Britain at this time was ruled by different **tribes.** Each tribe was divided into kingdoms with its own ruler, and these kingdoms often fought each other. War was part of their everyday life. Kings or queens would lead their army from a wooden chariot pulled by horses.

There were no towns in Britain, and no proper roads existed. People travelled on muddy paths or along rivers. Most people lived on farms. Houses were made from mud and wood with straw roofs.

This map shows where the tribes lived at the time of the Roman invasion.

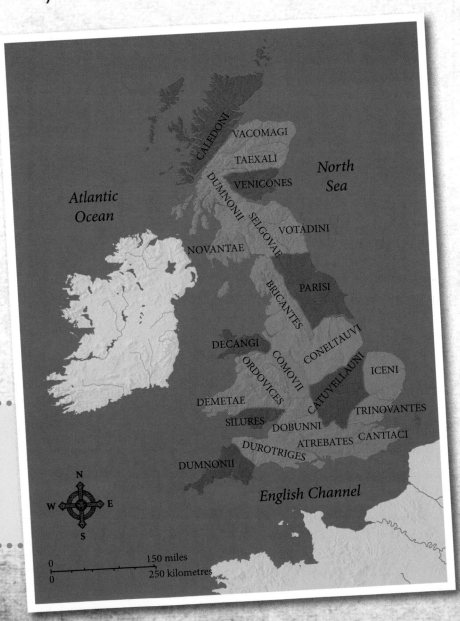

4

Bronze and Iron Age Britons were skilled at metalworking. This ancient British helmet is made of bronze.

Metalworking

The time before the Roman invasion was known as the Iron Age. The people who lived in Britain before the Romans invaded were the Celts. While some Romans, including Caesar, may have thought the Celts were savages, they had excellent metalwork skills. They made decorated weapons, jewellery and coins from different metals, particularly bronze and iron.

ARCHAEOLOGISTS

Archaeologists dig for objects from the past. They use these objects to find out more about people or places from long ago. We know where the tribes of Britain lived because of the coins that have been discovered in different parts of the country. Each tribe placed a picture of their ruler on one side of the coins.

TIMELINE

The Roman invasion and settlement of Britain happened over a number of years. This timeline will help you see what happened when.

For an explanation of what AD and BC mean, please see the glossary on page 30.

55 and 54 BC
Julius Caesar **invades** Britain

AD 43
Claudius invades Britain

AD 47
The first Roman town is built in Britain – Colchester, known to the Romans as Camulodunum

AD 60/61
Boudicca leads a **rebellion** against the Romans

AD 75-77
Wales surrenders to the Romans

AD 84
The Romans win a battle against the northern British **tribes**

AD 105
The Romans give up on the idea of **conquering** Scotland

AD 122
The Romans build Hadrian's Wall in the north of England to mark the edge of their **empire**

c. 270
The Romans start to build the Saxon Shore **fort** system around the southeast coast

360s
The Picts and Scoti (Irish) begin to attack Britain

397
The Roman commander Stilicho comes to the aid of Britain, helping to fight the Picts, Scoti and Saxons

409
The Britons push out the remaining Roman officials and decide to fight alone

410
The Romans leave Britain

476
Fall of the Roman Empire

Invasion

In 55 BC, Caesar and his army crossed the English Channel from Gaul, which is now known as France. This invasion of Britain was not successful because the Celtic **tribes** fought together to defeat the Romans. A year later, Caesar tried again. When his army did not win quickly, he decided Britain was not worth a long war and returned to Rome.

In AD 43, the army of Roman Emperor Claudius **invaded** Britain, led by Aulus Plautius. This army was well trained, well organized and the best in the world. The Romans landed in the south of Britain and soon defeated the Catuvellauni tribe. Claudius himself arrived in time to lead the army into Colchester, but he only stayed in the country for 16 days.

CLAUDIUS

Claudius was born in Gaul in 10 BC. He became Roman emperor in AD 41. Claudius was not known as a great soldier as many emperors were, but he is famous for **conquering** Britain. He died in AD 54, possibly as a result of being poisoned.

Client kings

After the invasion, many Celtic tribe leaders agreed to
obey Roman laws and pay money so that they could
keep control of their lands. These leaders were known as
client kings. One of these was Cogidubnus, ruler of the
Atrebates in southern Britain. It is thought that the Roman
palace of Fishbourne in West Sussex was built for him.

Boudicca's rebellion

Not all leaders were happy to accept Roman rule, and **rebellion** broke out regularly. One of the best-known rebellions was that of Boudicca in AD 60 or 61. Boudicca was married to the king of the Iceni, a **tribe** that lived in what is now Norfolk. After Boudicca's husband died in AD 59, the Roman emperor decided he wanted the Iceni lands. As well as taking the land, the Romans attacked Boudicca and her daughters.

Boudicca and the Iceni decided to rebel. Other tribes, including the Trinovantes, joined Boudicca. They fought against the Roman army while the Roman **governor**, Gaius Suetonius Paulinus, was in Wales. One **legion** was defeated, and the Celtic tribes went on to burn down the Roman capital Colchester, London and possibly St Albans too.

LAYERS OF ASH

Archaeologists have found layers of burnt ash in the earth of London and Colchester. This ash is proof of Boudicca and her army burning down buildings in these important cities.

Defeat

Suetonius Paulinus returned from Wales. His army met Boudicca's and defeated it easily. The tribes had brought their families to the battle, but they were killed by the Roman soldiers. Thousands of Boudicca's army died. Boudicca is thought to have killed herself with poison.

Everyday life

While people who lived in the countryside may have seen little difference to their lives during Roman rule in Britain, others saw much greater changes as they took up Roman ways and **customs**.

Remains of the Roman forum and basilica can be seen at Caerwent. The forum was the meeting area and the basilica was a law court.

WHAT'S THE LANGUAGE?

The names of some places in Britain come from Roman times. For example, -chester comes from the word *castrum*, which means **"fort"**. Places like Colchester or Chester were military towns in Roman Britain.

Verulamium (St Albans) was one of the largest Roman towns in Britain. Its amphitheatre can still be seen today.

Towns

The Romans built towns that had criss-crossed streets, high outer walls and gates. Instead of buildings made of wood and mud, they built them from brick, stone and tiles. Roman towns often had an **amphitheatre** where people could watch entertainment such as plays, or men called gladiators fighting each other. They also had baths where people could go to get clean or meet for a chat.

Caerwent, known in Roman times as Venta Silurum, is an example of a Roman town in south Wales. The town was built after the Romans had defeated the Silures **tribe** in around AD 70. It had a strong outer wall, much of which is still in place today. Inside the town walls could be found temples, public baths and large houses owned by wealthy people, called villas.

Keeping clean

Keeping clean was very important to the Romans. Baths were to be found in every Roman town, including those in Britain. Britons soon loved the baths as much as their **conquerors**. Rich people sometimes had their own baths at home, but poorer people went to public baths. Public baths had at least three rooms, each heated to a different temperature.

Aqueducts were bridges built on arches with a dug-out channel on top that carried water over long distances. The Romans built them to carry water into towns and cities. The aqueducts were sloped downhill so the water from a lake or river would be carried towards the towns and cities.

Some baths, like these in the city of Bath, took advantage of natural hot springs. These were important to a **tribe** called the Dobunni even before the Romans arrived.

Sewage systems

Sewage systems and underground drains were also brought to Britain by the Romans. Only the rich could afford drains to take away dirty water or toilet waste from their homes, but towns and **forts** made use of these systems. Water from the public baths was used to flush the drains.

Keeping warm

The hypocaust system was the Romans' way of keeping their houses and baths warm. A floor would be built on top of brick or tile pillars. Fires were lit underneath this floor and kept going by slaves. The heat would move through the tunnels made by the pillars, heating each room.

Sometimes the floor got so hot in public baths that bathers had to wear wooden sandals or they would burn their feet!

Roads

In order to keep Britain under control, the Romans needed an easy way to travel, so they built roads to replace the muddy tracks that people used before. Most roads were very straight and led to or from Londinium, Roman Britain's capital city from about AD 65. The roads were built on clay, chalk and gravel, and were sloped so that rain would run off into ditches at each side of the road.

Blackstone Edge, on Rishworth Moor near Manchester, is one of the finest surviving examples of a Roman road.

THE VINDOLANDA TABLETS

Over 400 **tablets** found at the Vindolanda **fort** in Northumberland reveal a lot of information about everyday life, including food. The tablets were made of very thin wood and date from AD 97–103. The tablets were letters written by Roman soldiers and their families who were living at the fort.

Food

The Romans brought new foods to Britain, including vegetables such as cabbages, onions, peas and leeks. Wine was also introduced by the Romans.

Wealthy Britons were able to try many new foods after the arrival of the Romans.

Other new ideas

The Romans brought many other new ideas to Britain, including education. Children of wealthy people in Roman Britain would have had lessons at home with tutors. Most other children did not go to school at all. The Roman system of law dealt with how to keep the peace and how to punish someone if he or she broke the law. The Roman calendar was created by Julius Caesar, the man who first **invaded** Britain in 55 bc.

Culture and leisure

Celtic art used lots of curving lines and patterns. Sometimes it showed animals and people, but Roman art showed the human body in a much more realistic way. Romano-British art mixed the two styles together. It was used for statues of gods and goddesses as well as for decoration. Copybooks were made that included pictures of Roman art for people to copy. Some Celtic people used these copybooks to learn from, which mixed the styles even more.

This mosaic floor is in Bignor Roman Villa in Pulborough, West Sussex.

Mosaics

Mosaics were common in Roman Britain. Many mosaic floors have been found in Roman villas. Rich people could choose what they wanted their mosaics to show. Less wealthy people could buy mosaics that were already made.

WHAT'S THE LANGUAGE?

The Romans spoke Latin, and wealthier Britons chose to learn it too. However, many Britons continued to speak British. Not many Latin words remain today, but Latin has had a huge influence on the English language. The words wall (*vallum*), candle (*candela*), and belt (*balteus*) are ones that were used by soldiers and merchants.

Leisure

What little spare time Roman Britains had, they spent playing board games or sport, or watching plays at the **amphitheatre.** Another popular pastime of the Romans and rich people was hunting. The Romans brought fallow deer to Britain especially for this purpose.

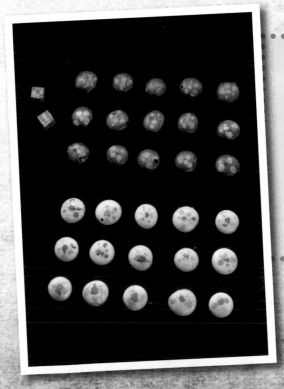

These dice and counters were found at Lullingstone Villa in Kent.

War

The Roman army was organized, well trained and had better weapons than any other army at the time. Roman soldiers were also paid. The army was powerful enough to defeat and then control countries over a vast **empire**. When they came to Britain, they brought new methods of fighting, such as the use of catapults and machines called ballistas that could shoot spears or large stones.

These actors are dressed as Roman soldiers. They are showing how to use a ballista.

WAYS OF FIGHTING

One of the **tablets** found at Vindolanda (see page 16) includes a Roman soldier complaining about the difficulties of fighting the Celtic people. "The Britons are unprotected by armour ... The cavalry do not use swords, nor do the wretched Britons mount in order to throw javelins." This soldier did not like the way the Celtic people would not stand and fight face-to-face like the Romans. The armour worn by Romans allowed them to fight face-to-face because they were better **protected**.

The metal plates of a legionary's armour helped protect him. Legionaries carried shields as well as their weapons.

Legionaries and auxiliaries

Roman soldiers were divided into **legions,** which were groups of 3,000–6,000 men. The soldiers were known as legionaries. They were helped by soldiers called auxiliaries who came from the countries that had been **conquered.** By about AD 100, there were 50,000 Roman troops based in Britain. The army did not just help to keep the peace, they also built roads and **forts.**

Defence

Romans knew that it was important to be able to defend your kingdom or country from attackers. In the north, soldiers had to defend against Picts from Scotland and the Scoti from Ireland.

Hardknott Roman fort in Cumbria was built by the Romans in the early AD 100s. These are the ruins.

Hadrian's Wall

After the Emperor Hadrian visited Britain, he decided to build a wall to mark the outer edge of Roman Britain and help defend against attacks from the north. The building of the wall began in AD 122 and took about six years to complete. Roman soldiers guarded the 117-kilometre-long wall at **milecastles**. Milecastles were built at every Roman mile, which was about 1,500 metres. Major **forts** were built at about every 8 kilometres.

EMPEROR HADRIAN

Hadrian was born in Rome in AD 76. During his time as emperor (AD 117–138), Hadrian was known for travelling throughout the Roman **Empire**. He was the emperor who stopped the empire from getting any bigger, building walls, such as the one in northern Britain, to mark the edge of the empire. He died in AD 138.

Saxon Shore forts

From about AD 270, the Romans built forts to **protect** the east and south coasts. These forts have become known as Saxon Shore forts because people from Northern Germany called Saxons were the main attackers.

Religion

Both the Celts and the Romans followed religions that worshipped many different gods. The Romans often accepted the gods of the people whose countries they **conquered**. This helped to keep the peace. When the Romans arrived, they simply joined the Celtic gods with their own gods – whichever were most alike. Sulis was a Celtic goddess of healing and was linked to hot springs. Her name has been found on stone inscriptions at the Roman baths in Bath. The Romans joined Sulis with their goddess of wisdom, Minerva. However, some Celtic gods and goddesses, such as Coventina, remained local.

COVENTINA

Gods and goddesses were worshipped at temples or **shrines**. At Carrawburgh on Hadrian's Wall, a shrine to Coventina has been found. Coventina was a goddess of healing and childbirth. There is a well at the centre of the shrine. More than 13,000 Roman coins and other items of worship, such as pearls and carved stones, have been found inside the well. These were offerings to Coventina.

Statues and images

Celtic people did not make statues of their gods. When the Celts saw the Roman images of gods and goddesses, they copied them. This meant that Celtic gods and goddesses were often made in a Roman style or shown with both Celtic and Roman decoration.

The head is all that remains of a large bronze statue of the goddess Sulis Minerva, discovered in the Roman city of Bath.

Protection

Superstition was important to the Romans at this time. Some people wore pieces of jewellery, called amulets, which were often made of protective materials such as jet or amber. They hoped these would **protect** them from evil. People asked gods for good luck or for help with particular problems. People also put **curses** on other people for revenge, or if they didn't like them.

This wall painting at Lullingstone Roman Villa contains the Christian symbol of Chi-Rho.

CURSE TABLETS

Lead curse **tablets** have been found in the hot springs at the Roman baths in Bath. These tablets often contain written reports of crimes, particularly theft of money or clothes. For example, the writers ask for help from the goddess Sulis to punish the thief by not allowing them to sleep. This punishment will only stop when the stolen money or goods are returned to their owner or given to the goddess.

This statue of Emperor Constantine sits outside York Cathedral.

Christianity

In York in 312, Emperor Constantine announced that **Christianity** was the new Roman religion. However, **archaeologists** have not found much proof that many Britons became Christians at this time. A bowl with a Chi-Rho symbol has been found in London. A Chi-Rho symbol is the first two letters of Christ's name in Greek. Lullingstone Roman Villa in Kent has some of the earliest examples of Christian belief in Britain. The Christian wall paintings there date from about AD 350.

The end of Roman rule

Roman rule in Britain lasted for more than 350 years. In that time, certain parts of the country and some groups of people saw a big change in their lives. A system of straight roads was created, which allowed people to travel more easily. New foods were introduced and **hygiene** was improved. Even the name of the country – Britain – came from the Romans.

It is difficult to know exactly what the Celts thought of these Roman ideas and inventions because few people could write at that time. Most of what we know about what happened during the years of Roman rule has come from Roman writers such as Tacitus and Cassius Dio. For example, the names of the Celtic **tribes** come from what the Romans called them.

Hadrian's Wall in Northumberland is one of Britain's most famous Roman sites.

Before the Romans arrived, the tribes fought amongst themselves. The Romans actually brought the country together. Many British people wanted to become Roman citizens, although others probably continued to live the same way they had always done.

The Roman palace of Fishbourne in West Sussex had 100 rooms! Many of them had **mosaic** floors, like this one.

The Anglo-Saxons

Towards the end of Roman rule in Britain, tribes from northern Europe began to attack the country. These tribes later became known as the Anglo-Saxons. It was they who formed the next ruling group in Britain.

Glossary

AD dates after the birth of Christ; these count upwards so AD 20 is earlier than AD 25

amphitheatre outdoor theatre with seats rising on curved rows around it

archaeologist person who studies objects from the past

BC dates before the birth of Christ; these count downwards, so 25 BC is earlier than 20 BC

Christianity religion that teaches about the life of Jesus Christ

conquer take control of an area or country by force

curse request for a god or goddess to harm a particular person

custom particular way that a group of people behave or do things

empire countries under the rule of another country

fort building that can be defended against an enemy

governor ruler

hygiene keeping clean

invade take over a place or country by force

legion group of 3,000–6,000 soldiers in the Roman army

milecastle small, rectangular fort

mosaic picture made from many small pieces of coloured glass, tile or stone

protect to keep someone from harm

rebellion fight against a ruler or ruling group

shrine place of worship

superstition beliefs that are based on fear of the unknown, or magic

tablet flattened piece of wood or stone used for writing on

tribe group of people with the same language and customs

Find out more

Books

Life in Roman Britain (A Child's History of Britain),
   Anita Ganeri (Raintree, 2014)
Roman Britain (100 Facts), Philip Steele
   (Miles Kelly, 2008)
Roman Britain (History on Your Doorstep), Alex Woolf
   (Franklin Watts, 2012)

Websites

www.bbc.co.uk/schools/primaryhistory/romans
This BBC website has lots of information about the
Romans.

**www.bgfl.org/bgfl/custom/resources_ftp/client_ftp/
ks2/history/boudicca**
This website tells the story of Boudicca's revolt from four
different viewpoints, including Boudicca's.

Places to visit

If you want to visit some of the places mentioned in this
book, such as the Roman baths in Bath or Hadrian's Wall,
tind out more at the following websites:

The Roman Baths, Bath
www.romanbaths.co.uk

The National Trust in England, Wales and
   Northern Ireland
www.nationaltrust.org.uk

English Heritage
www.english-heritage.org.uk

Index